Y0-AQV-151

SccerAtEase

A guide to success in soccer
[and in the larger game called life]

By

Lawrence Fine

Published by The Writers' Collective
Cranston, Rhode Island

SoccerAtEase
A guide to success in soccer
[and in the larger game called life]
by Lawrence Fine

Copyright 2003. Lawrence Fine

*All rights reserved. No part of this publication may be
reproduced, stored in a retrieval system or transmitted
in any form by any means electronic, mechanical,
photocopying, recording or otherwise, except brief extracts
for the purpose of review, without the permission
of the publisher and copyright owner.*

ISBN: 1-932133-43-7

Library of Congress PCN NUMBER: 200209656

Printed in the United States of America

Published by The Writers' Collective
Cranston, Rhode Island

Acknowledgements

I would like to thank Barry Gorman for his wonderful 'success pyramid' which forms a supplement to this book. His language is simple and easily understandable, laced with interesting quotes.

I would like to thank Chris Bahr for his encouraging foreword. Chris has been two time Super Bowl Champion, Rookie of the Year in the NASL and a success in Professional Soccer, Law and Business. His kind words of appreciation mean a great deal to me.

Also, I would like to thank the wonderful people at www.virtualjeeves.com who helped with the editing, graphics, layout and design of SoccerAtEase. Without their help (and friendship), this book would never have been finished.

I would like to also thank all of the wonderful people I have met over the years through soccer without whom, my life would have been very different. Many of these people were willing to help read through rough drafts of this book and make comments and suggestions.

Lastly, I would like to thank you, readers, for taking the time to read through SoccerAtEase, hopefully learn from it, and pass this knowledge on to others. Though this book has been written with reference to success in soccer, you will realize that it applies equally to success in the bigger game of life.

As always, have a great day!

Lawrence

Foreword

SoccerAtEase is a story that should prove invaluable to coaches and players from all sports. Lawrence Fine has taken Barry Gorman's "Personality Pyramid" and explained it in an easy to read story. Unlike most manuals with their endless diagrams and tactical discussions SoccerAtEase had me rushing from section to section. I wanted to find out who the next guest player would be.

During my years in professional sports I have seen numerous talented players. When you have two players with similar talent, why does one excel and one languish in mediocrity? Often times it is the "intangibles" that make the difference. Coach Gorman's "Personality Pyramid" helps coaches and players alike identify those intangibles.

As a coach you can't teach these traits. You can only encourage and challenge your players to do what is necessary to set them apart from the masses. As a player you need to be honest and ask yourself if you are going the extra mile to be, as they say in the US Army, "the best you can be."

Travel with the Futopians, with SoccerAtEase at the helm, on their journey to the "light at the end of the tunnel."

Chris Bahr

The Kick-Off

The people of Futopia had a dream - to produce a world-beating soccer team. After all, this little-known town boasted of some of the best-known soccer stars in history. In fact, old Futopians still recall the day when the visiting world champions were beaten 2-1 by the home team in a friendly match. Currently too, it had a good team, but it was fading. So the Futopians decided that a whole new team should be created, one with every winning quality in the textbook.

Fifteen of the most promising youngsters of Futopia
were handpicked by the local coach. They were
taught every trick, trained in every technique.

"The goal is near," exclaimed a senior citizen and
a Futopian fanatic, who watched them play.
"These boys would soon put our name back on the
world soccer map and restore our pride,"
he said in a voice choked with emotion.

But were the Futopians battle-ready?
Well, it didn't appear so, going by their performance
in the state-level league matches.

What was going wrong? The boys had the stamina
and the skill, technique and the talent.
But something was missing.

"Why don't we consult SoccerAtEase?"
one of them suggested.

*SoccerAtEase. No one knew his real name.
His adventures on and off the soccer field and his
wisdom had earned him the nickname. There are
some, though, who believe that SoccerAtEase is his
real name and he is a direct descendent of the great
Greek philosopher with a similar sounding name.
SoccerAtEase was older than anyone could guess,
but the soccer champ in him was active and kicking.*

*So the Futopians invited the wise old man of soccer
to witness one of their games, evaluate their
strengths and weaknesses, and light up
their path to success.*

SoccerAtEase, after an initial round of long discussions, during which he asked plenty of questions, said finally to the team, "The power to win is within you. I may teach, and yet you may not learn. So, the only way to learn the secrets of success in soccer is to live them, experience them and imbibe them. I can just facilitate that."

The Soccer guru spoke with the authority of an expert and the temperament of a mystic.

Using his influence, which was known to be very high in the soccer circles, he got the State Champs, the Invincibles, to visit Futopia and participate in a series of practice matches during a two-week coaching camp (SoccerAtEase preferred to call it a learning camp) to be followed by a challenge match, that would decide whether the boys had indeed become men.

The first match between the Futopians and the Invincibles was not a match. It was a massacre of a bunch of talented soccer players by a strong, well-knit team of opponents. The game plan of the Invincibles was not extraordinary but it had a well-laid, clinical approach towards the 90-minute task.

From the very first moment of the kick off, the Invincibles took possession of the ball and retained it for a large part of the game. Their players had better understanding of each other; they ran on the field with aim and achieved a resounding victory in the end. The Invincibles raided the Futopian team's goal again and again; almost all their players scored in the game.

The Futopian players showed equally good skill on the ball - trapping, passing and dribbling - but they lacked something that was essential for winning. They could not win the ball back from their opponents' feet; they lost possession of the ball many times through interception by the Invincibles; most of their passes went begging for connection; they shot wide and aimlessly.

At the end of the match, it was a sad story of the Futopian team losing by a margin of 0-15, a crushing defeat by a team of opponents who were superior in all departments of the game. On the contrary, nothing went right for the Futopian team.

The 0-15 defeat was a lesson of their lifetime.

*After the match, as the Invincibles were celebrating
their win, the Futopians decided to have a session
with their Facilitator, SoccerAtEase and analyze
the day's game.*

*Paul, the Captain of the Futopian team, was the
first to speak.*

*"What do you think went wrong today?"
he asked SoccerAtEase in total exasperation.*

*"What do **you** think went wrong today?"
the guru responded, throwing the question
back at no one in particular.*

*A stony silence followed for almost a couple of
minutes. "We made some basic mistakes," admitted
Moses, the midfielder. "We didn't combine well
as a team, perhaps?" queried Paul.*

"Can you explain that one?" SoccerAtEase asked.

Responses started pouring in.

"Our attack lacked cohesion."

"We squandered our chances in the penalty area."

"We gave up too easily and too often"

"We really wanted to win, but..."

"That's the point. It all boils down to the DESIRE to win", summed up SoccerAtEase. No one around could have missed the gleam in his eyes.

"Are you suggesting that we didn't have the desire to win?" asked Antony, stung by the suggestion. "Whoever plays without the desire to win?"

The voice of SoccerAtEase took on a sharp note. "Do you agree, in the first place, that desire is important to win?"

The answer was a unanimous "Yes".

"If that were so, who out of any two teams with the desire to win would eventually win?"

Paul spoke for everyone when he replied. "The one with the greater desire to win."

*"Tomorrow, I shall invite an eminent personality
to join our team as a guest player,"*
said SoccerAtEase.

"He will impart in you the desire to win."

"Friends, Futopians and Soccer fans," SoccerAtEase
began, exuding confidence, *"I have the greatest
pleasure in introducing to you a man who
symbolizes the desire to win.*

*"A man who asks not what his team can do for him,
but what he can do for his team.
Ladies and gentlemen, please welcome
John Fitzgerald Kennedy."*

*Amid loud cheers and ecstatic shouts,
John Kennedy led the Futopians into the field.
And the second day's play started.*

The Desire to win

To the disheartened members of the Futopian team, the evening appeared all set for yet another thrashing by the visiting team. But SoccerAtEase thought otherwise. He looked hopeful and confident, mainly due to the new addition to the team: John F. Kennedy.

JFK was bubbling with enthusiasm, as others watched him with a blend of curiosity and cynicism. The next 90 minutes brought them a revelation.

JFK, playing the position of striker, exhibited verve and vigor, and an insatiable desire for taking the game into the opposite end.

After ten minutes of play, he stole the ball from the feet of the opponent's midfielder and surged ahead at a moderate speed looking on either side for back-up. He had none, and hence started running into the wall of defense. He lost the ball in the crowd but was still trying to regain possession. The Invincibles' big defender blocked him physically and the ball rolled sideways to be taken away by one of the opponents. Yet, no one from the Futopian team was on the spot. They were still ambling all over the field. The ball reached them a couple of times, but accompanied by three opponent attackers. The disjointed defense ran everywhere except in the path of the ball which was neatly buried inside the net. Four more goals against the Futopian team followed.

Only the newcomer, JFK, with the burning desire for success, had made some spectacular raids into the rival area. No back-up for JFK and no score for the Futopian team.

The second half saw more onslaughts by the opponents, many of which were allowed by the jittery defense of the Futopian team to be converted into goals. On the few occasions when the Futopian team had the ball, there were glimpses of good technical skills which fell short of resulting in a goal.

By the 60th minute, the opponents had converted three corners. One headed in by a tall defender who took a high cross near the far post. Another low corner kick was deflected into the legs of Futopian defender who couldn't stop the ball from rolling in. And the third came from a glancing header from a running opponent.

By now, the Futopian team members began
the notorious negative style of play, back passing
to their goalkeeper repeatedly and keeping
possession of the ball for minutes together inside
their own half. They were trailing by 0-9 and were
terror-stricken. They failed to take notice of
the courage and spirit showed all along by their
new colleague.

JFK was still toiling hard, surging ahead whenever in
possession of the ball. He was communicating well
with his teammates in the language of soccer but they
failed to comprehend his messages. He proved a real
threat to the opponents who were otherwise
comfortable throughout.
He made direct aggressive runs towards them;
made diagonal runs up to the goal posts on either
side hoping for a support down the middle.
During the last few minutes, he was indeed able to
have a sight of the opponent's goal and even had
a crack at it from a decent distance.

Nothing bore fruit. Yet, JFK's desire for scoring, taking his game into the opposite camp and coaxing his teammates to join his forays never subsided during the entire 90 minutes.

The final result was 0-12.

But yet, a laudable performance from JFK. An occasion to remember and learn from.

John Fitzgerald Kennedy was the youngest man ever elected President of the United States and the youngest ever to die in office.

In his inaugural address, he declared that a new generation of Americans had taken over leadership of the country. He said Americans would "... pay any price, bear any burden, meet any hardship, support any friend, oppose any foe to assure the survival and success of liberty."

Kennedy won world respect as the leader of the Free World. He greatly increased United States' prestige when he turned aside the threat of an atomic war with Russia while forcing the Russians to withdraw missiles from Communist Cuba.

He formed the Peace Corps, which carried his enthusiasm to the people of developing nations to help them raise their standards of living.

On the domestic front, the US enjoyed its greatest popularity in history. During Kennedy's administration, the United States made its first manned space flights and prepared to send astronauts to the moon.

Kennedy was a war hero. He received the Navy and Marine Corps Medal for his heroism and leadership. He was also awarded the Purple Heart for being wounded in combat.

Kennedy's life represents his burning desire to serve his country.

John F. Kennedy
(1917 - 1963)

"Desire is where it all begins," summed up
SoccerAtEase, after the game. *"Desire must be
a genuine, heart-felt, gut-wrenching emotion flowing
from your very being. And, as JFK showed today,
it must be demonstrated through actions and deeds."*

"We played better today, but we still lost the match,"
observed Paul in a tone that combined bitterness
and frustration.

"Time for introspection again!" said SoccerAtEase.
*"Playing better isn't good enough. You've got to be
the best you are capable of being."*

Had this profound thought come from anyone other
than the guru, Paul would have reacted differently.
For now, he managed a grin.

SoccerAtEase continued, *"Let me explain.
Do you believe you gave JFK the kind of support
you should have given?"*

The philosopher's strategy worked. The question provoked a volley of responses.

"No, we didn't."
"Anticipation. I suppose that was lacking."
"We just waited for things to happen."
"We didn't really press on."

"Precisely," SoccerAtEase beamed,
"You didn't persist. You lacked the..."

"DETERMINATION?" Moses, the midfield specialist, completed. "Yes," said SoccerAtEase, "and when you have the desire and the determination..."

"You win," Moses said with a wise expression.

"No," said SoccerAtEase, "you get started."

"Tomorrow, I shall invite a renowned personality to join our team as a guest player," said SoccerAtEase.

"He will impart in you the determination to win."

"Here's a man who can take our game a quantum leap forward," announced SoccerAtEase. "A man who symbolizes determination. Please welcome Albert Einstein."

An air of anticipation filled the stadium as Albert Einstein led the Futopians into the field.

And the third day's play started.

The Determination to win

On day 3, the Futopians had the benefit of a guest player who was full of determination - Albert Einstein. He was positioned at left back. He ran smoothly but with a hard target in mind; the back of the opponents' net. He was a class defender too.

All the members of the Futopian team were endowed with sufficient skills and physical abilities. What they were presented with during the match was something exemplary. Einstein was determination personified.

He exuded determination in tackling the incoming opponents - never allowing them to bypass him, and meanwhile trying his hardest to pluck the ball from their feet. He succeeded on all occasions except two. He chased the advancing opponents as if his life depended on the fate of the ball and cleared the ball to safety before it was struck into the goalmouth. He proved more than a match for the opponent attackers. Not only in guarding the fort but also in carrying the attack forward,

Einstein was relentless - trying harder and harder. But the Futopian team failed to be inspired by him.

The opponents went on a goal- scoring spree, netting one after another at regular intervals.

Impatience prevailed on a few occasions resulting in a penalty kick goal in favor of the Invincibles and in one yellow card for the Futopian team. The thrashing continued and the half time score read 5-0 in favor of the Invincibles.

Undaunted by the huge margin, Einstein was as mobile as ever, running down the flanks, sending crosses in front of the opponent's goalmouth. No one dared to come near him when he was on guard in defense. All the attacking moves from the opposite camp came down the other flank or the middle.

There were signs of 'desire to win' emanating from his teammates but they were not sufficient to check the marauding opponents. The Futopians lacked in determination, a quality exhibited abundantly by Einstein.

The scorecard read 10-0 at full time.

A complete demolition of the Futopian team
except for one player - Einstein.

He was undoubtedly the best player of the day.

The Futopian team failed, but the day was a success,
for it provided them with an opportunity to witness
a live display of determination, and to experience
its importance.

Albert Einstein, best known for his theory of relativity, was one of the greatest scientists of all time.

He displayed the trait of determination at a very young age: he would never give up on building card houses several stories high and would keep going on and on.

Einstein's theory of relativity, developed through deep philosophic thought and complex mathematical reasoning, laid the foundation stone for the development of atomic energy.

The photoelectric cell or "electric eye" resulted from his work in quantum theory and made possible sound motion pictures, television and many other inventions. He received the 1921 Nobel Prize in Physics for his work on quanta.

Einstein spent the last 25 years of his life working on a 'unified field theory' but failed to establish it; he remarked that it would be worthwhile to show that such a theory did not exist.

Einstein was a champion of the underdog, never concerned about money. His determination, concentration and perseverance should be a lesson to all those who wish to break new ground in scientific discoveries.

Albert Einstein
(1879-1955)

"You may not have quite made it, but you are on your way," observed SoccerAtEase, after the game.

"That's very encouraging," said Paul sounding as polite as he could. *"Are there any more traits we need to acquire?"*

"Quite a few," answered the wise man, his enthusiasm unabated. *"But, let us tackle them one at a time. For example, once you set your eyes on the goal, aim for it unswervingly."*

"I remember what Harvey Mackey said," interjected Moses, in an attempt to lighten the mood. *"Be like a postage stamp. Stick to it until you get there."*

"Now tell me, when you desire something, when you are determined to be successful, what should you do to achieve it?" asked SoccerAtEase.

The answer was a chorus: "Everything."

"Everything! And I have a word for it: DEDICATION," concluded the wise man of soccer.

"Tomorrow, an acclaimed personality will join our team," said SoccerAtEase.

"He will impart in you the dedication to win."

"In today's match, our team will have a man who is matchless," SoccerAtEase announced dramatically. *"A man who symbolizes the dedication to win. Ladies and gentlemen, meet Edson Arantes do Nascimento, known to you all as the great Pele."*

The eager crowd continued to swell as Pele led the Futopians into the field.

And the fourth day's play started.

The Dedication to win

The Futopian team which seemed to head nowhere on the opening day had, by now, incredibly changed direction, thanks to the morale-boosting and inspiring display of soccer by the two guest players. To further uplift the Futopian team, another guest, Pele, arrived to play as the right striker.

The way Pele approached the day's play revealed the quality of dedication inherent in him. The initial minutes of the first half certainly belonged to the strong and methodical opponents. But one man began to retaliate by making scorching runs on his own towards the Invincibles' goal.

His dedication prevailed over the arena for
90 minutes and the strong opponent team had to find
new methods to stop him from bypassing them on his
raids. After all, one man can cover only a small area
on the vast soccer field.

The Invincibles' first goal came from the left winger
who took the ball straight to the wing half, tapped it
gently between his legs and picked the ball up to
show a clean pair of heels to the defenders coming
across from the middle. He ran to the left flag post,
lobbed the ball above the goalkeeper's head,
saw the ball touch the far post and go in.

A neat goal and an indication of what was to follow.
The opponents scored 9 times, each a clinical
dissection of the Futopian team save the one man,
Pele, who played like a true warrior, with fierce
dedication, fighting a mighty army of opponents to
the end to score the only goal for the Futopians.

With one or two associates with the same dedication, it appeared that he might have changed the score sheet in favor of the Futopian team.

Three goals were scored from scrambles in front of the goalmouth. Of course, the Futopian team showed a remarkable improvement on their desire and determination to play well. They played with more vigor and spirit, sometimes leading to overindulgence which led them nowhere. Some decisions of the referee also were against the Futopian team which seemed to shorten their temper. But Pele took everything in his stride, played with calm composure and exhibited a rare quality of dedication that began to receive some attention from his teammates.

He showed them the wonders dedication can bring
to a hard-running, tough-tackling game of soccer.
The scorecard that read 9-1 was not an indication
of what Pele, the new player with the synonym
'dedication', brought unto the Futopian team players.

Edson Arantes do Nascimento or Pele is one of the greatest soccer players of all time. He scored 1,281 goals in 1,363 games during his professional career.

He set the soccer field ablaze with stunning poise, balance, rocketing speed, and shooting skills. His father taught him football and his father's foot injury made him play football to support his family.

Pele shot with both his head and foot and was a charismatic, talented footballer. He set several records and represented Santos, his home club. Once a cease-fire was effected in a war in Nigeria for 2 hours so that everybody could watch Pele in action.

Pele, also called the 'Black Pearl', has an astounding record for the maximum number of goals and has scored multiple goals numerous times.

Once Muhammad Ali said of him when he met him that there were two of the greatest, not just one.

Pele is a lover of children and would never tire of signing autographs. His love for soccer was close to religious and nothing less. He once said: "It seems God brought me to Earth with a mission, to unite people and never to separate them."

Pele
(1940 -   )

"Today, we shall talk about a quality that has to do with self-image and self-satisfaction," SoccerAtEase began. "A quality that must come from within."

"Sir, I am a simple soccer player. Could you give me a simple explanation?" Paul pleaded.

"You must train yourself to do the right thing at the right time," clarified the philosopher. "You must have DISCIPLINE. That's what will give your passion a purpose."

"Tomorrow, I shall invite a distinguished personality to join our team," said SoccerAtEase,

"He will impart in you the discipline to win."

"Today's guest is a larger-than-life man who symbolizes discipline," said SoccerAtEase, "A man who has nothing to offer but blood, toil, tears and sweat. Ladies and gentlemen, please welcome Winston Churchill."

"Will fortunes turn in Futopia's favor?" the audience wondered, as Churchill led the Futopians into the field.

And the fifth day's play started.

The Discipline to win

Only four days had passed, but some incredible things had happened to the Futopian team's soccer. All the members of the soccer team had begun to show signs of confidence and zeal for better performance. Three of the essential qualities - desire, determination and dedication - had been wonderfully portrayed by the three guest players. And the Futopians had imbibed much of these qualities by now. Day 5 brought yet another quality player with yet another quality - discipline.

The newcomer, Churchill, was playing at a back position and was in a class of his own in positioning himself for the ball and in creating chances for other teammates. He made some scintillating runs down the line each time, sending perfect tailor-made crosses.

In case the ball got lost on play, he would be the first to retreat and reach his actual position, ready to smother any attack coming through. He would automatically fill the gaps left by his moving teammates in defense. His efforts failed to bring victory for his team but his message reached everyone.

The Invincibles' attack came in waves. A well spread pattern of attack involving all midfielders and strikers, using short passes, return passes, body joints that showed better coordination and a well-laid plan of attack. Their endless raids culminated in 7 goals.

The Futopians were a different set of players with the recently acquired qualities of desire, determination, and dedication. They put up a stern fight but missed opportunities to score. An inner strength that had built up inside the Futopian team was visible in their spirited approach to the game.

In the end, though they lost the game 7-0, they had gained something more valuable – the quality of discipline.

Sir Winston Churchill, one of the greatest statesmen in world history, reached the height of his fame as the heroic Prime Minister of Great Britain during World War II.

His sense of discipline, generosity of spirit and leadership qualities made him indispensable for Britain in its greatest hour of crisis.

Churchill's service started in 1895 under Queen Victoria and ended in 1964 under Queen Elizabeth II, the great-great-grand daughter of Queen Victoria -- perhaps the longest of its kind. The roller coaster political career was marked by joys and sorrows, successes and failures. But Churchill combined boundless energy, tremendous physical endurance and great sensitivity to tide over every trial and emerge triumphant.

Churchill first came to national limelight after his daring escape from a prison in Pretoria, during the Boer war, when he was a war correspondent.

His strong sense of discipline and courage continued to inspire the nation in good times and bad.

This larger-than-life man had combined so many roles: soldier, leader, statesman, orator, author and painter. He was awarded the Nobel Prize for his 6-volume history of World War II.

Sir Winston Churchill
(1874 - 1965)

"Would one of you like to sum up what we've learned till now?" asked SoccerAtEase.

"The four D's," answered Moses, springing to his feet, "Desire, Determination, Dedication and Discipline. The formula for success."

" Not quite," said SoccerAtEase. "The four D's form only the foundation for success. We are now ready to move up from the 'D' level to the 'C' level."

There was genuine pride on everyone's face. Hope had triumphed over despair.

"At this level, I have 3 intangible qualities for you," SoccerAtEase continued. "You would have observed that we are steadily moving from qualities that make a player complete, to qualities that set him apart." The soccer philosopher was in his element.

*"Today," he continued, "we'll talk about a quality
that will set you apart as an individual, and also
make you blend in with your team. A quality that'll
help you understand each other better."*

*"I understand," said Paul, the captain.
"Communicating among ourselves."*

"Yes, but not just verbal," clarified SoccerAtEase.

"The rapport," said Moses.

*"The CHEMISTRY?" ventured young Billy.
"My girl friend keeps using that word."*

*"The first C," said SoccerAtEase,
with an approving nod.*

"That's what binds us together," the Coach was
the next in the chain to react.

"Very true," added Paul. *"Without effective
chemistry, there's no way to be effective in a team."*

That's chemistry at work, SoccerAtEase
said to himself.

"Tomorrow, I shall invite a celebrated personality to join our team," said SoccerAtEase.

"He will impart in you the chemistry to win."

"Soccer was never so entertaining," exclaimed SoccerAtEase. "Here's a man whose chemistry with his fans virtually rocked the world. Ladies and gentlemen, please welcome Elvis Presley."

The audience prepared to witness yet another clash between experience and exuberance, as Elvis Presley led the Futopians into the field.

And the sixth day's play started.

The Chemistry to win

Defeat had not dampened the Futopian spirit,
SoccerAtEase noted with pride,
as his boys marched in.

The Futopian team, after the five enlightening
matches, had now begun to look ahead. They had
inherited the four basic qualities of desire,
determination, dedication and discipline founded
on which their soccer will grow, they now realized.
SoccerAtEase had introduced them to a new kind of
soccer - a blend of technicalities and mental qualities.

On this day, they had a guest player with a captivating personality and an effervescent smile. So far, the Futopian players had never been able to communicate on field. Shouts went unheard because of the deafening noise around the field. Gesticulations were not possible always. Mutual understanding and coordination eluded them on all previous matches.

The new guest player, Elvis, sprang a surprise on them. He was able to communicate to all his teammates throughout the match. Whatever he thought, whatever move he planned, whatever he expected of the other players, all reached the Futopians instantly. He mixed his soccer movements with his body language beautifully which enabled him to take his game to them and make them his partners.

Elvis played as the right midfielder. He was the pivot from whom passes evolved. But, his teammates were not always there to receive them in time.

More often, Elvis went on his own making direct runs at the opposition. He hit the cross bar with a long ranger once from 25 yards and chipped the ball once over the advancing goalkeeper to score his first goal.

On several occasions, he made diagonal passes, both low and waist high, to his right and left, but his half backs didn't connect the ball even though they were running hard.

The right back of the Futopian team showed a lot of determination to take the ball to the opposite end. He made perfect crosses, one of which was met by a strong header into the bottom of the net by Elvis as if he was waiting for the cross. He seemed to have guessed every move of his teammates. He never failed to join them in attack and in defense.

Once, when the Futopian goalkeeper was out of his goal and when his teammate unknowingly back passed, Elvis charged in to clear the ball to safety. The strong opponents scored as many as 6 times but the Futopians scored only once. In the end, the result didn't look discouraging to the Futopians because, Elvis had exhibited a very rare quality in the team game - the quality of chemistry that connects players.

Elvis Aaron Presley, the king of Rock 'N' Roll, was the most popular American singer in the history of rock music. His 'chemistry' with his fans is unparalleled. On stage, initially, he adopted sexually suggestive movements that excited teen-agers. Later, he recorded songs with slower rhythms and more traditional melodies, which won popularity with older audiences as well.

Elvis, who was also a black belt in Karate, lived only till 42 years of age. By then he had given more than 1100 concert performances and sold millions of records. For a number of years, he was one of Hollywood's top box office draws and one of its highest paid actors.

The US Postal Service issued the Elvis Stamp, which is the most widely publicized stamp issue in history and the top selling commemorative postage stamp of all time.

What most people do not know is that Elvis Presley gave away most of the millions of dollars he had earned to charity. Today, there are some 625 active Elvis Fan Clubs worldwide. His recordings and films continue to enjoy popularity all over the globe. His home in Memphis has become a major tourist attraction visited by thousands of fans.

Elvis Aaron Presley
(1935 - 1977)

"*The Invincibles didn't look all that invincible today,*" observed Paul, confident despite defeat.

"*Well, the gap is certainly closing,*" said SoccerAtEase generously. And then he asked "*Why do you think we lost the game today?*", looking into the eyes of each player for an answer.

"*Beats me,*" said Moses, shaking his head.

"*Me, too,*" said the coach. "*Everything about our game was good. Tireless running, tidy passing.*"

Billy cut in "*And we never took chances.*"

"*There's your answer,*" exclaimed the philosopher with piercing eyes. "*You didn't go for the shots when you should have. You were perhaps concerned about being blamed for missing it. You lacked COURAGE.*"

"Tomorrow, I shall invite a reputed personality to join our team," said SoccerAtEase.

"He will impart in you the courage to win."

"Get ready for a game of soccer with a lot of punch,"
said SoccerAtEase as he introduced the guest to
the audience. "Ladies and gentlemen,
please welcome Muhammad Ali, a man
who symbolizes courage."

Expectations soared, as Ali led the Futopians
into the field.

And the seventh day's play started.

The Courage to win

Muhammad Ali came in as left striker of the Futopian team. He exuded confidence. He was fearless in running into defensive walls in front. Shirt pulling and tough tackling opponents didn't bother him.

The Futopian team was playing well in many departments of the game. They had acquired new qualities that made a big difference to their soccer.

But, qualities such as desire, determination, dedication, discipline and chemistry were not enough.

To tackle strong and big players, to run into a host of defenders with the ball needed much of courage that appeared non-existent among the Futopian players.

Only on this day, Day 7, the players were able to sample the quality of courage as displayed, in its full glory, by Ali. He got the ball from the middle, attacked down the line on the left. He was never troubled by the opponents' right half sidestepping him. He made life tough for the defender at right back, first cutting across to the middle into the charging defenders. He was shouldered hard and pulled by hand. He was still going when someone collided with him; he didn't mind. He burst towards the goal. The goalkeeper lunged at his feet.
But Ali lobbed the ball ahead before going down with the goalkeeper. The whole team of defenders could not stop him.

What was important was that Mohammed Ali was unperturbed by the numerous collisions, trippings and pushing duels with the opponents. He was playing with a single purpose - to score and win, never bothering about any possible injuries.

The Futopian team had, by now, acquired a rhythm of its own. It scored once as against
5 times by the opponents. It had learned to restrict the opponents' score but was yet to strengthen and vitalize its own attack. It still lacked certain qualities that guarantee the ultimate victory.

Muhammad Ali became the first heavyweight champion to win the title four times. He is also one of the most colorful and controversial champions in boxing history.

Born Cassius Marcellus Clay, he learned boxing to get back at a schoolmate who stole his bicycle. He became a professional boxer after winning the light heavyweight title at the 1960 summer Olympic Games. He later converted to the Muslim religion and changed his name to Muhammad Ali.

In the ring, Ali "floated like a butterfly and stung like a bee." His fights with Sonny Liston, Joe Frazier and Leon Spinks are legendary.

Ali is a man of exemplary courage. He remained brave despite defeats and being stripped of his title by the WBA. He bragged about his ability and, often, even predicted the round in which he would defeat his opponents.

He had charisma and the crowds flocked to see his bouts. After the terrorist attacks of Sep 11, Ali made public appearances to denounce the cowardly attacks.

Today Ali is battling with Parkinson's disease. But he courageously makes public appearances and raises funds to feed the poor and hungry.

He was honored in the 1996 Olympics by being asked to light the flame.

In his own right, Ali is a world hero.

Muhammad Ali
(1942 -   )

"Today," SoccerAtEase said, "we'll talk about a quality that will set you apart as an individual; help you become a better soccer player, a better sportsperson and a better human being. I am talking about CHARACTER, my friends."

"Character is what you are in the dark," Moses couldn't resist recalling a quote he had read.

SoccerAtEase was actually impressed. "It is indeed. It's the moral quality that controls your life – and your game."

"But is it as important as physical skills to win a game?" queried Billy, the youngest in the team.

"Without Character, your foundation for success will collapse," said SoccerAtEase.

"Tomorrow, I shall invite an illustrious personality to join our team" said SoccerAtEase.

"He will impart in you the character to win."

"The spirit of Soccer can never be contained," began SoccerAtEase. *"And you're about to see it for yourself. Please welcome a man who symbolizes character: Nelson Mandela."*

Defeat had not dampened the Futopian spirit, SoccerAtEase noted with pride, as Mandela led the Futopians into the field.

And the eighth day's play started.

The Character to win

The Futopian team had come a long way.
They showed a phenomenal improvement in their
performance. They were acquiring newer qualities and
maturing into a well-knit, better organized team.
Their mental capacity was on par with that of their
well-known ball skills. They looked all set to equal the
state champs in every quarter, yet something was
amiss which was still costing them a victory on field.

The match on Day 8 brought to them a fine
display of Character, that eluding quality,
by the guest player, Nelson Mandela.

He played as the left midfielder who was to support every move from the central area. What made him stand apart was his inherent quality of Character.
He was enjoying every moment on the field.
He had an enigmatic smile on his face -
a contradiction in a tough game like soccer.
He never fouled his opponents. He took their dreadful tackles with sporting spirit.

When, in the closing minutes of the first half, the referee awarded a penalty kick to the Futopian team, Mandela calmly went to the referee and explained that he slipped and fell; no one tripped him down.
He showed this character of sportsmanship on quite a few such occasions. At the same time, he initiated many moves and inspired his teammates. This was a cool, composed approach to the game, underlined with a genuine love for soccer and the passion to win.

He possessed such a strong character that no setback
during the 90 minutes diminished his spirit for
playing quality soccer. He was passing
the ball at the right moment to the right person.
When, in the second half, he went close to scoring
with only the goalkeeper to beat, which
didn't appear difficult, he nudged the ball to his right
for the right striker who was close on his heels to
volley in home. He showed how to use the best
available moment to the best advantage.
His character of camaraderie, clinical approach
to the match and sheer love for soccer put him above
the rest of the players.

The Futopians were able to note his characteristic
display but were unable to adapt it then and there.
But they played a far better game. They nullified many
attacks on their goal. Yet the opponents won by 4-I.

Nelson Mandela, a great leader and human rights activist, symbolizes a rare strength of character and grit.
He became the President of South Africa after spending 27 years in prison.

From an early age as student, Nelson disliked racism in all forms and took part in several student uprisings. He wanted the cruel apartheid regime to end and the equality of blacks to be recognized. Mandela finished his studies in law and set up a law partnership firm with one of his close friends. The government posed barriers by banning his practice in urban areas and by striking his name off the list of attorneys. But Mandela overcame all these hurdles.

He faced many trials and was sent to prison several times. He started guerilla training groups in Algeria in 1962. Sometimes he had to move around in disguise to avoid being recaptured, and for this he was called the "Black Pimpernel".

Mandela never wavered in his campaign or changed his ideals. The government came half way with offers to make him give up his fight but he rejected them outright: an eloquent testimony to his character and uprightness.

Almost every country has honored and felicitated him. He was awarded the Nobel Peace Prize in 1993.

Nelson Mandela
(1918 -   )

"Welcome to 'B' level," SoccerAtEase greeted the team, visibly impressed by their remarkable performance, at the end of the day's play.

And he quickly went on to draw a diagram on the ground using a twig.

When he had finished, it looked like a triangle to the guys.

"It's a pyramid," he said, sounding as if he had read their minds. "A Pyramid of Personality Traits, to be precise. At the bottom, the 'D' level, we have four blocks: Desire, Determination, Dedication and Discipline. Above that, at the 'C' level, we have 3 blocks: Character, Courage and Chemistry. That brings us to the two qualities at the 'B' level, the first of which is..."

"Excuse me," young Billy butted in. "Why don't you also tell us, as we go along, which of these is more important?"

"That's exactly what I was leading you to,"
said the master patiently. "BALANCE, the first of
the two qualities at the 'B' level."

"We need all of them in the right proportion,"
said Billy, sounding enlightened.

"Tomorrow, I shall invite an outstanding personality to join our team," said SoccerAtEase.

"She will impart in you the balance to win."

"She?" Billy wasn't sure he heard it right.

"Yes. And let me warn you, she is so fast that if you blinked, you'd miss her."

The Balance to win

Eight days of enlightening soccer had skyrocketed the performance level of the Futopian soccer team. The team owed it to their respected coach and his guest players. They now realized the inherent human potential that has to be brought out in performance. SoccerAtEase had singled out each trait that combined to evolve a successful soccer team and had presented them with a live demonstration of these qualities through successive matches. Yet he was not satisfied. Today, he had brought in a goalkeeper.

Wilma Rudolph, the new goalkeeper, became an instant sensation. There are two types of goalkeepers - those who play according to their reflexes and those who play according to anticipation. Rudolph belonged to the second category. When the ball was on the edge of the area in the initial stage of the match, and someone hit it long, it was difficult to guess whether it was a goal attempt or a forward pass to be connected. But Rudolph anticipated well, stood rooted to her guard and collected the overhead ball calmly. She never panicked. She passed a low shot from the opponent's most powerful strikes.

The opponents, the State Champs, began to elevate their game further when the Futopians managed to restrict them to a lead of just 1-0 at half time. They got a free kick in a promising position but the mercurial goalkeeper moved like lightning and punched the ball with tremendous power. Likewise, she thwarted numerous attempts, which might have been sure goals otherwise.

Another curved shot came in, a beautiful one; again
a good block by the goalkeeper. She was cool,
displaying steely nerves and brilliant anticipation of
the flight of the ball. She personified a spirit
that is vital for a winning team.
She seemed to have inspired her dedicated teammates
and was aided well during difficult moments.

The State Champs managed a 2-0 win,
having been denied a big score by Rudolph,
the new goalkeeper. Their goals were coming from
scrambles close to the goalmouth.
All long rangers, straight or curved, were saved with
aplomb by the calm Futopian goalkeeper,
Wilma Rudolph. Her balance in everything she did
was astonishing. The Futopian players could
recognize a special quality in her soccer.

Born premature, the 20th of 25 children in a poor African-American family, and stricken with double pneumonia, scarlet fever and polio which virtually crippled one leg, Wilma Rudolph was the most unlikely baby to grow into an athlete.

Incredibly, the sick kid from Clarksville overcame her ailments to become one of the world's most celebrated women athletes of all time. The first American woman to win 3 gold medals in one Olympics [100-meter and 200-meter dash and the anchor on the 400-meter relay team in Rome in 1960].

Her achievements not only set many records but also broke gender barriers in previously all-male track and field events. A victory parade was held in Wilma's honor, which was the first racially integrated event in her hometown. This was followed by more honors including the Black Sports Hall of Fame, the US Olympic Hall of Fame and the National Women's Hall of Fame.

Wilma Rudolph symbolized a perfect balance of courage and perseverance, grace and generosity, elegance and exceptional calm. She created a Foundation to help young athletes, worked as a university coach and served as a goodwill ambassador to West Asia.

' The Black Gazelle' died of brain cancer in 1994 at the age of 54. Her life continues to inspire young athletes, the world over.

Wilma Rudolph
(1940 - 1994)

"You were so good, you threw your opponents off balance," SoccerAtEase complimented the Futopians.

"Thanks to your guidance," Paul said with genuine reverence. *"Initially, cynicism had blurred my vision. But now, I am beginning to see the road to victory quite clearly."*

"That's the beginning of the next quality at the 'B' level: BELIEF," noted the inimitable philosopher. *"Belief in yourself. Belief in your teammates. I am sure Moses would like to add to this."*

"Mahatma Gandhi," Moses responded with enthusiasm. *"He said 'I can. It's a powerful sentence. I can.'"*

"Yes, we can," said Billy. And then the others repeated, one by one. *"Yes, we can."*

"I believe you," said SoccerAtEase.

"Tomorrow, I shall invite a legendary personality to join our team," said SoccerAtEase.

"He will impart in you the belief to win."

"Fasten your black belts," advised SoccerAtEase,
*"and witness the feet of fury. Friends, with us today
is a man who symbolizes belief: Bruce Lee."*

"Will this be the turning point?" the audience
wondered as Lee led the Futopians into the field.

And the tenth day's play started.

The
Belief
to win

From a poorly performing congregation of eleven soccer players, the Futopian team had grown astoundingly into a well-organized unit of strength and spirit. From the past few days' matches, they had acquired the vital ingredients of success: the qualities of desire, determination, dedication, discipline, chemistry, courage, character and balance.

Today, SoccerAtEase had brought in Bruce Lee to play as right back. Their regular no. 5 was showing undue hesitation to spot an opportunity and was prone to hasty, aimless clearances.

Lee displayed a rare sense of faith and confidence in his teammates and in himself. His belief in their soccer, in their every move and in their capabilities was total.

He was calm and composed in his tackles, snatching the ball from the opponents' feet, and holding on to it by dribbling a few strides and making perfect long passes to his attack line. He never stood rooted to his post of defense but was seen marauding down the flank.

A free flowing runner with the ball, Bruce Lee made several crosses of which two were met by his teammates successfully. He himself scored from a long range shot from the top of the penalty box. He took a swerving free kick that the expert goalkeeper just managed to push out with an outstretched hand. He was sometimes fouled against, but he never lost his temper. Bruce Lee was proving to be a real threat to the strong State Champs.

The ball was shifted to the other flank where it was either misplayed or lost. Lee began switching over to the central field once he reached the opposite half, thereby heading closer to the ball. Despite the poor passes and failed attempts at scoring, the Futopian team was playing better, looking better.

The new guest player, Lee, had a staunch belief in all that is soccer and in his capabilities which he demonstrated in a fitting manner by leading the Futopian soccer team to a heart-warming performance. Of course, they lost by 1-2 but they had an eye-opener in the performance of Lee whose belief in everything he did was transparent throughout. They were unable to adapt it on field but they took notice of the quality of belief, which proved to be vital to the praiseworthy performance of Lee.

Bruce Lee became one of the greatest exponents of martial arts. He practically defined the fledgling martial-arts movie genre. His athletic skills seemed almost superhuman. He is applauded for the postulation of 'Jeet Kune Do', an innovative martial art system,which is still developed and practiced in the USA.

Bruce Lee's family lived in Hong Kong and, when he was 18, moved permanently to the USA. A philosophy major from the University of Washington, Lee entered show business in the mid 1960's.

He made several movies depicting his stunning skills as a martial art exponent. These include "The Orphan", "The Fist of Fury", "Enter the Dragon" and "Return of the Dragon". He lived a short energetic life. Bruce Lee never did standard stunts like breaking boards, which he felt had nothing to do with martial arts.

He was a man who believed in himself and who, by virtue of his rigorous back-yard training, had reached phenomenal heights.

In his own words, "Training deals not with an object, but with the human spirit and human emotions."

Bruce Lee
(1940 - 1973)

"It's only appropriate that as your performance reaches its peak, we reach the peak of the pyramid," began SoccerAtEase.

"Interestingly, the tenth trait, at the 'A' level, is one you'll acquire easily when you have the other nine, namely: Desire, Determination, Dedication, Discipline, Character, Courage, Chemistry, Balance and Belief.

"It's this 'A' that guides your thinking and actions. Any guesses?"

"ATTITUDE!" the response was instant, unanimous.

"I think it's an Indian proverb," said Moses trying to recollect the source. "We can't direct the wind, but we can control our sails."

"Try this," said the Coach. "It's not the position. It's the disposition."

"Tomorrow, I shall invite a towering personality to join our team," said SoccerAtEase.

"He will impart in you the attitude to win."

*"Today marks the end of our learning session. And,
the beginning of a new chapter in Futopian soccer,"
declared SoccerAtEase. "To lead our team to the
peak of the personality pyramid, I invite
a man who symbolizes the power of attitude:
Abraham Lincoln."*

*Amidst deafening cheers and ecstatic screams,
Lincoln led the Futopians into the field.*

*And play on the eleventh and final day of
the practice matches started.*

The Attitude to win

From the bottom of the rungs in soccer, the Futopian team had slowly and steadily climbed to a level almost on par with their opponents.

Their players had received a first hand demonstration of nine qualities essential to soccer. In this match, Lincoln would show them what Attitude, a quality that towers over the rest, means in soccer.

The match started in a silent atmosphere, for the spectators had now realized the fact that the Futopian team was no longer a pushover. Lincoln took the position of left striker.

For the next 90 minutes, he not only made run after run, but also created waves of attack from the entire Futopian team.

He was dynamic in moving on and off the ball.
He played as if the Futopian team will get a scoring opportunity every minute of the match. He was never part of any negative play.

Many times his raids were frustrated by the State Champs. All members of the Futopian team were playing well - adhering to their posts, keeping the ball in possession for a longer duration, defending well, conducting themselves well; still they were trailing. Unlike the earlier matches, the match on day 11 resulted in a low score with both the teams playing technically well.

The Futopians were nearly matching the far more experienced and extremely well trained state champs, thanks to Lincoln. He was so impressive that his teammates, now with their newly acquired wisdom, could make out something special in the guest player.

And when the match ended in a draw, at 1-1, the Futopians were more than delighted. No one felt the need for a post-match analysis on this day.

Abraham Lincoln, the sixteenth President of the USA, was one of the truly great men of all time, celebrated for his kindly spirit and selflessness. He could rise to each new challenge. He was a master politician, and timed his actions to the people's moods. He led his people by persuasion. His insight, clarity of expression and iron will helped the North win the civil war and preserve the Union.

Lincoln rose from a humble origin to the nation's highest office. He grew up on a frontier farm, educated himself by reading books and worked as a general store clerk, before his positive attitude carried him to success and recognition. He made extraordinary efforts to attain knowledge. His law partner said of him, "His ambition was a little engine that knew no rest." Sharp-witted, he was not especially sharp-tongued, but was noted for his warm good humor.

Lincoln is most often remembered for freeing American slaves and delivering the Gettysburg address, the most famous oration in American history.

Abraham Lincoln
(1809 - 1865)

SoccerAtEase delivered his 'now famous' address to Futopians before the Senator's wife kicked off the Challenge Match:

"This is a significant moment for Futopia. And, by the end of the evening, I am confident, it would become a historic moment as well. Every day, over the past eleven days, there has been a change in the way Futopians have played, and every change has been an improvement. Our boys are all set to restore the Futopian pride.

"Call it a test of nerve or a tryst with destiny, the Challenge match tomorrow will be remembered for a long, long time.

"Victory to Futopia!
Know thy soccer, know thyself!"

The Challenge Match

The stadium thundered with chants of 'Futopia, Futopia', as the heroes marched into the field to fulfill their mission. What followed was more than a spectacular display of skill, speed and stamina. It was a revelation of the power within each one of them. The Desire to win, the Determination to perform, the Dedication to persevere, the Discipline to inspire, the Character to lead, the Courage to dare, the Chemistry to involve, the Balance to control, the Belief to succeed and the Attitude to excel.

In a reversal of roles, the Futopians raised the game to a new level. The final score of 2-0 in their favor doesn't fully reflect the fire, passion and artistry of the young champions. Of course they had one big advantage;
an invisible extra player who combined the qualities of Kennedy, Pele, Einstein, Churchill, Mandela, Ali, Presley, Wilma, Lee and Lincoln.

The disciples of SoccerAtEase won the match, the hearts of their supporters and a place in history.

*Toasts were raised and tributes were paid to
Invincibles, 'the friendliest foes', for bringing out
the best in the Futopians; to the eminent guest
players for raising the level of the game and the
inimitable SoccerAtEase for his 10-step guide
to success in soccer.*

*Futopia took on a festive look. Thousands of ecstatic
enthusiasts poured into the streets dancing and
singing, celebrating the historic victory. Some made
eloquent speeches; some shed tears of joy and a few
were lost in a speechless trance.*

A Futopian ideal had been realized.

Footnote:

The Futopians have gone on to win every match they played at the league level as well as the national level. Look out! You may spot some of the stars of Futopia at the next World Cup.

The Personality Pyramid has been made a subject of compulsory study in the Institute of Soccerology. Industries are adopting it to boost employee morale and it is becoming an important lesson in life skills, the world over.

As for SoccerAtEase, the call of duty and the cause of soccer have taken him to another distant small town of soccer maniacs.